# Whodunnit

# Law Enforcement

C.M. Johnson

Law Enforcement
Origins: Whodunnit

Full Tilt Press
42982 Osgood Road
Fremont, CA 94539
www.readfulltilt.com

Full Tilt Press publications may be purchased for educational, business, or sales promotional use.

**Editorial Credits**
Design and layout by Sara Radka
Edited by Lauren Dupuis-Perez
Copyedited by Renae Gilles

**Image Credits**
Alamy: Don Klumpp, 17, Niday Picture Library, 20; Getty Images: Chip Somodevilla, 33, Darren McCollester, 43, Jake Schoellkopf / Stringer, 31; Newscom: 6, EPA, 13, 41, Everett Collection, 26, 38, Picture History, 9, 28, Stapleton Historical Collection/Heritage-Images, 4, UPI, 29, UPI/Chris McGathey, 19, WRATHER PRODUCTIONS / Album, 23, ZUMAPRESS/Barry Sweet, 39, ZUMAPRESS/Michael A. W. Evans, 27, ZUMAPRESS/Michael Goulding/The Orange County Register, 40; Shutterstock: Axenova Alena, 37, BartlomiejMagierowski, 36, Everett Collection, 7, 14, 18, 24, 25, Joseph Sohm, 30, Nagel Photography, 11, Stocksnapper, 10, Stuart Monk, 44, W. Scott McGill, 15; Vecteezy, background and cover elements; Wikimedia: Beland, 8, DOJ, 35, Historian Insight, 21, U.S. National Archives and Records Administration, 34

ISBN: 978-1-62920-613-4 (library binding)
ISBN: 978-1-62920-625-7 (eBook)

Printed in the United States of America.

# Contents

# BEAT COPS

Like British police, early American forces rode horses. Today, the New York and Los Angeles police departments still use mounted officers.

# Introduction

In early America, small groups of people lived far apart from one another. But even these small groups needed law and order. The first police were Native American warriors who kept order on hunts. The first European settlers used **peer pressure**. In rural areas, people all knew one another. If a person caused trouble, their neighbors told them to stop. Everyone kept their eye on strangers.

Once towns were created, early settlers had watchmen. These men walked the streets. They reported fires and broke up fights. Some were paid a fee by private citizens. Others volunteered. In the early to mid-1800s, cities grew. **Immigrants** poured in. Watchmen could not keep track of everyone. Crime rose, and "Yankees" clashed with the new citizens. Yankees were from England and the Netherlands. Their families had arrived earlier. They were not sure they liked the new German and Irish families, who had new **customs**. Many of the new immigrants followed a different religion than many of the Yankees. The Yankees called for ways to control the newcomers. One way was by creating public police forces.

**peer pressure:** influence from other people in a group or community

**immigrants:** people who come to a country to live there

**customs:** practices or acts common to a particular group of people

In the late 1700s, much of the land surrounding Hillsdale, New York, consisted of wild forests and farmland. The Van Rensselaer family claimed to own most of it.

# The Moment

The first officers in America had to take sides in fights. This meant risky work for the police. In 1791, people were fighting over land in Hillsdale, New York. A group of farmers said they had bought their land from Native Americans. But a rich Dutch family, the Van Rensselaers, said it was theirs. They said they would sell or rent the land to the farmers, but the farmers would not pay. The law upheld the claim of the Van Rensselaers.

On October 22, 1791, Sheriff Cornelius Hogeboom rode out to Jonathan Arnold's farm. He was going to tell Arnold he had to leave. Arnold knew he was coming, and Hogeboom walked into a trap. Arnold gave a signal. Seventeen men jumped out. They were covered in war paint. They shot Hogeboom, and he died from his wounds. On October 31, the governor of New York issued a reward to catch the men. He said this kind of "mob justice" must not win. In February of 1792, the men were charged with murder and brought to trial. But the jury was on their side. The men were found not guilty.

**DID YOU KNOW?**

In 2011, Sheriff Hogeboom was honored by the National Law Enforcement Officers Memorial Fund as the first American officer to die in the line of duty.

Many people were angry about how the Hillsdale landowners treated farmers. Because of this, some jurors may have sided with Hogeboom's murderers.

# History of Order

In the United States, community policing has a history that spans hundreds of years.

## 1631

A year after the city of Boston is founded, the first watchmen are established there.

## 1647

Watchmen begin walking the streets of New Amsterdam, later called New York City.

## Early 1800s

Large numbers of immigrants from Germany and Ireland settle in Boston and New York City.

## 1845

The first public police department is formed in New York City.

## 1846

In Boston, just 30 officers and 150 watchmen patrol a city of 140,000 people.

**1852**
Police departments are established in New Orleans and Cincinnati.

**1848**
Boston police watch officer David Esters tries to stop two burglars. He is shot and killed. Other officers arm themselves with pistols for the first time.

**1854**
Official police departments are established in Boston and Philadelphia.

**1900**
The Boston Police Department now has 1,000 officers in its ranks.

**2013**
There are more than 12,000 local police departments in the United States, employing about 605,000 officers.

Between 1820 and 1846, immigration from other countries caused the population of New York City to grow from 100,000 to 500,000.

# The Spread of Justice

By the 1830s, New York City was crowded. The city was on an island. Space was limited. People from many countries were living right on top of each other. They were often poor. They were competing for jobs. They also spoke different languages. These factors led to many misunderstandings. Gang members from different countries shot one another in the streets. The governor of New York asked the state for help. He wanted an official police force to help keep order. In 1845, the force was created.

Other cities were facing the same issues. In 1851, Chicago created its own force. In the next few decades, other cities did the same. People argued over what these forces should do. Some rich people wanted the police to keep order, no matter what. Others worried about this policy. They did not like the methods police used. The cops beat up workers who went on **strike**. Often, they targeted immigrants. Cities like Boston worked to prevent these abuses. The city hired cops from the community, including immigrants. They also hired a high number of officers. This way, each cop could work a **beat**. A "beat cop" walked around a small area of the city. They got to know the people who lived in the neighborhoods they patrolled. This created more trust on both sides.

**strike:** a protest in which a group of workers stop working in order to get their employer to agree to their demands

**beat:** police terminology that means a territory and time that a police officer patrols

## Blue Laws

In the 1800s, cities across America argued over "blue laws." These were laws that restricted activities on Sundays. Yankees often pushed for these laws. They thought Sunday should be a day of prayer and rest. They wanted businesses to be closed. They did not want a lot of noise. Many Irish and German people had different ideas. For them, Sundays were for sports and music. The police were often caught between these two beliefs. In some cities, blue laws still exist today.

# Living Within the Law

In America today, we face many of the issues we did in the 1800s. Populations are changing. People move here from places like Africa and the Middle East. The police must find translators so they can speak to new immigrants. They must learn about new customs. They must **negotiate** between new and old citizens. Officers often face fear and **bigotry**, even within their own ranks.

But cities like Boston have a tradition of community policing. In 2013, two bombs went off at the Boston Marathon. Three people were killed. More than 200 were injured. For four days, the two suspects were at large. People were scared. Would they strike again? The Boston Police Department kept in touch with the public on social media. They gave updates, corrected mistakes made by the press, and reported road closures. They also helped people turn in pictures and videos from the race. All of these things helped police find and eventually capture the bombers. In 2014, three professors in the criminal justice department at Harvard University praised the Boston police. They had made the search a public effort. They had kept people calm. They had built trust. The professors urged police forces everywhere to follow Boston's example.

**negotiate:** to try to solve an issue in a way that is acceptable to everyone

**bigotry:** hatred or intolerance toward the members of a particular group

### DID YOU KNOW?

Every year, the Boston Marathon is held on Patriots' Day, a holiday that honors the two battles that started the Revolutionary War in 1775.

The Boston Police Department's response to the 2013 bombings has helped create a friendly relationship between marathon runners and officers.

# TEXAS RANGERS

The early companies of rangers were often outnumbered by as many as 50 to 1.

# Introduction

You might spot Texas Rangers by their gray or white Stetson hats. You might also see stars pinned to their coats. Today, the Texas Rangers are a **prestigious** division of the Texas Department of Public Safety. But they are best known for their Wild West roots.

The first Texas Ranger badges were made out of Mexican coins by jewelers, gunsmiths, and metalworkers.

In the 1820s, Stephen F. Austin was in charge of bringing settlers to Texas. However, he could not keep the new settlers safe. Local Native Americans were mad. They were losing their land. They were fighting back. **Bandits** were also a threat. In 1823, Austin created a "ranging company" of men to protect his settlers. These men did not wear uniforms. They rode their own horses. They shot their own guns. They were not paid very much. At times, they were not paid at all. Most of the time, they stayed at home. But when there was a threat, these rangers rode out to fight.

### DID YOU KNOW?

In the 1820s, Texas was not yet a state. It was a province of Mexico called Tejas.

**prestigious:** honored or having a high status

**bandit:** an outlaw who lives by stealing from other people

# The Moment

In the mid-1800s, John Coffee Hays was a captain in the Texas Rangers. He was known for his bravery. He had great skills as a tracker. He also brought in a new gun. This was the Colt revolving pistol. The pistol could fire five times before it had to be reloaded. Previous guns had to be reloaded after every shot. The Colt could give rangers an edge even when they were alone.

In 1841, Hays proved this in a big way. Hays was on patrol with his men in the Texas hills. All at once, a group of Native Americans called Comanches was upon them. Hays got separated from his men. He ran to a rocky hill. He took what shelter he could find there. He did not have much hope. But for hours, he held off the warriors by shooting his Colt.

Finally, when he was down to his last bullet, his men rescued him. The fight came to be known as "The Battle of Enchanted Rock." Legend says that the Comanche thought Hays had magical powers. Magic or not, Hays left a **legacy**. The Colt is a symbol of the Texas Rangers. Many of them use a modern version of the gun.

**legacy:** a quality or tradition passed on from one generation to the next

John Coffee Hays served in the Texas Rangers until 1846, and later went on to serve as sheriff of San Francisco County, California.

# History of Order

The Texas Rangers are more than a symbol of Texas law and order. They have also played a big part in the history of the state.

### 1835

Three companies of rangers are established, fifty-six men to a company. Official pay is set at $1.25 a day.

### 1823

Stephen F. Austin creates two companies of men to act as "rangers for the common defense" in Texas.

### 1836

Thirty-two men of the Gonzales Ranging Company volunteer to fight at the Alamo in San Antonio in a battle for Texas' independence from Mexico.

### 1874

The term "Texas Ranger" first appears in a legal document. This document creates the Frontier Battalion, made up of six companies of rangers. These companies are stationed around the state to help when ranches are raided by bandits.

### 1845

Texas joins the United States. Mexico declares war on the United States, and many rangers join the American army as scouts.

**1902–1920**

Rangers clean up crime in newly formed "oil-boomtowns" on the Texas prairie.

**1930s**

Women are given "Special Ranger" appointments to work in security at the governor's mansion in Austin.

**1935**

The Texas Department of Public Safety is created. The modern Texas Rangers are established as the main criminal investigative branch of the agency.

**1988**

Sergeant Lee Roy Young Jr. becomes the first African American member of the modern Texas Rangers.

**2014**

The Texas Rangers is made up of 134 commissioned officers organized into 6 companies.

Rangers used horses to quickly travel long distances and to fight in Texas's rugged hill country.

# The Spread of Justice

Stephen Austin first got the idea for a "ranging company" from the "Minute Men." These men fought in the Revolutionary War. A call for troops would go out. The men would drop their usual work of farming or running a business and go. After the battle, they would go back home. The Rangers also tried out the style of battle used in the Revolutionary War. They had **fife** players. They marched on foot. But this did not work well against Native American fighters galloping by on horses. Very quickly, the rangers got horses, too. They learned many lessons in these mounted battles. Their skills helped shape **cavalries** in the **Civil War** (1861–1865).

**fife:** a small flute often used in battle to give signals and orders to the troops

**cavalry:** the division of an army that rides horses

**civil war:** a war between groups of people in the same country

## Los Diablos Tejanos

During the war with Mexico (1846–1848), Mexican soldiers called the Texas Rangers *Los Diablos Tejanos*. This is Spanish for the Texas Devils. While some of the first rangers were known for their skills, others were known for being **brutal** and mean. American soldiers said that after taking over a city, some rangers stole livestock. They killed people for fun. In the 1840s, US General Zachary Taylor wrote that the Texans fought bravely. He was always glad to have them with him on the day of battle. But after the fight, he never wanted to see them again.

The rangers were creative. They could think and adapt quickly. They used the best tools they could find. In the 1920s and '30s, Ranger Manuel T. Gonzaullas worked in the oil boomtowns of Texas. These were rough places. They were filled with gamblers and drug runners. There was a lot of money. People would kill to steal it. But Gonzaullas liked to work alone. He was known as *El Lobo Solo*, the Lone Wolf. Gonzaullas used new scientific methods to catch **crooks**. He learned about fingerprints and blood tests. In 1935, he started the first crime lab in Texas, at that time one of the best in the nation.

**brutal:** extremely harsh or violent

**crook:** a person who gets what he or she wants in dishonest ways

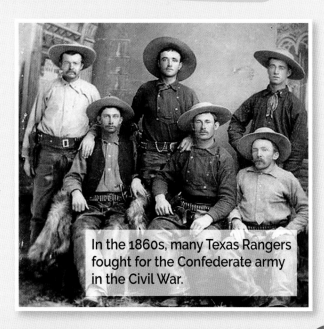

In the 1860s, many Texas Rangers fought for the Confederate army in the Civil War.

# Living Within the Law

In 1933, a radio show kept the Wild West ranger alive. Listeners heard a **fanfare** of trumpets. Then there were hoofbeats and a cry of "Hi-yo, Silver!" *The Lone Ranger* was born. In the story, a ranger chases the gang that killed his company. He wears a black mask. He rides a white horse. The show was a hit. In 1950, *Tales of the Texas Rangers* was popular, too. Each episode was based on a real case. The Texas Department of Public Safety read each script before it aired. Many of the stories were based on the work of Manuel "Lone Wolf" Gonzaullas. Later, both shows moved to television. The rangers have also inspired books like *Lonesome Dove*, by Larry McMurtry.

**fanfare:** a short and lively burst of music

**corruption:** dishonest behavior, especially of people in power

**recruit:** to encourage someone to apply for or to fill a position

Today, the Texas Rangers look into major crimes. These include cattle thefts and cases of public **corruption**. The rangers have strict requirements. Applicants must be officers in Texas. They need eight years of police experience. They must pass physical tests. Even though it is hard to join, the rangers are so popular that they do not need to **recruit**. Many Texans dream of joining the legend of the rangers.

Clayton Moore played the part of the Lone Ranger in *The Lone Ranger* TV series. It was on the air from 1949–1957.

President Theodore Roosevelt was protected by Secret Service agents at his second inauguration in 1905.

# Introduction

In the 1800s, the United States had a money problem. The issue was that much of it was fake. People were making copies of paper bills. By the end of the Civil War, nearly half of all bills being used were not real. In 1865, the Secret Service was created to fight the problem. Its agents still watch over US banks. They hunt down credit card thieves. They also protect our public water and power systems.

In 1901, Congress asked the Secret Service to take on another issue. This was the **assassination** of presidents. President William McKinley had been killed that year. He was the third US president to be murdered. Today, Secret Service agents are best known for shielding our leaders from threats. They look out for the leaders' families. They also protect visiting foreign officials.

The many **counterfeiting** operations in the 1800s made the public distrustful of US paper bills.

## DID YOU KNOW?

The counterfeiting of money is one of the few crimes mentioned in the US Constitution.

**assassination:** the murder of a person in a planned, secret attack, often for political reasons

**counterfeiting:** the process of making a fake copy of something of value

President Reagan waved to the crowd moments before he was shot. White House Press Secretary James Brady was also hit, and suffered partial paralysis as a result of his injuries.

# The Moment

It was March 30, 1981. President Ronald Reagan was two months into his first term. He gave a speech in a hotel in Washington, D.C. As he was leaving, six shots rang out. A man named John Hinckley Jr. had been waiting. He had a .22 revolver. A Secret Service agent, a police officer, and a White House staff member were hit. Another bullet ricocheted off the car waiting for the president. Agents Ray Shaddick and Jerry Parr pushed Reagan in. The car sped off. The agents breathed sighs of relief. Then, Reagan put a handkerchief to his lips. It came away soaked in blood. His face was very pale. Parr told the driver not to go to the White House. They had to get to a hospital. There, doctors found a bullet near Reagan's heart.

Luckily, Reagan lived. But the close call changed things for the Secret Service. Now, people are not allowed to get so close to the president without being scanned by a magnetometer. This device can help find guns. Tents are now used to shield exits and entrances. Training sessions for agents who protect the president occur more often. They train about two out of every eight weeks. This helps keep their instincts sharp.

## DID YOU KNOW?

At the hospital, President Ronald Reagan joked with his wife, telling her that he "forgot to duck."

John Hinckley Jr. said he tried to kill the president in order to impress the actress Jodie Foster.

# History of Order

The Secret Service has a long history of protecting the interests of the United States, including the safety of the president.

## 1867

The service's responsibilities expand to include investigations of crimes against the US government. Agents look into the Ku Klux Klan, mail robbers, and smugglers.

## 1865

The Secret Service is established as part of the Department of the Treasury.

## 1902

The Secret Service begins protecting the president full-time. Two officers are assigned to the White House.

## 1950

Private Leslie Coffelt is shot and killed while protecting President Harry S. Truman in Washington, D.C.

## 1951

Secret Service protection is expanded to the vice-president.

**1963**

President John F. Kennedy is assassinated in Dallas, Texas.

**1968**

Robert F. Kennedy, John F. Kennedy's brother, is assassinated while running for president. Congress then authorizes the protection of major presidential candidates.

**1975**

Two assassination attempts are made on President Gerald Ford in California. In the first, a Secret Service agent wrestles a shooter to the ground. In the second, agents push Ford into his car to avoid the shots.

**1970**

Phyllis Shantz is the first female officer to be sworn into the Secret Service division that protects the White House.

**2001**

The Secret Service establishes Electronic Crimes Task Forces across the country to fight high-tech criminals who use computers to steal money.

**2007**

In May, protection begins for 2008 presidential candidate Barack Obama, the earliest any candidate has started protection detail.

# The Spread of Justice

TV has made one type of Secret Service agent very familiar. These agents stick close by a leader's side. They wear suits and dark glasses. They look big and tough. But not every agent is on the president's security detail. Others work behind the scenes. They work with local and state police to secure events. They track **identity fraud**. They hunt down foreign spies.

**identity fraud:** using someone else's personal information illegally, usually in order to get money

Agents who are part of the president's Counter Assault Team provide cover in case of an attack. They wear heavy combat vests and carry high-power rifles.

How does one get into the Secret Service? The first step is to look in the mirror. Are any tattoos visible? Tattoos on the head or hands must be removed. Then it is time for tests and background checks. Secret Service hopefuls will be interviewed many times. They will take lie detector tests. Agents must make sure applicants can be trusted. Agent trainees then head to the Federal Law Enforcement Training Center (FLETC) in Glynco, Georgia. General training lasts several months. Then specialized training begins. These courses last 14 to 18 weeks. Trainees might learn how to spot counterfeit money. They might learn how to physically protect someone. They might learn first aid or study international law. Special agents often begin work in a field office. After six to eight years, they might serve in a protective assignment that lasts three to five years. Then an agent returns to an office in the field.

### TRAINING

At FLETC, students use a wide range of facilities. Weight rooms and gyms help them get in shape. Being physically fit makes tough training exercises easier. They practice their skills in crime labs and mock court rooms. They learn to shoot on 18 different firing ranges. Many types of federal law enforcement members are trained there. FLETC works with agencies like the US Forest Service and the Bureau of Indian Affairs.

# Living Within the Law

Over time, the duties of the Secret Service have changed. Often the changes were sparked by events. In 1963, when President John F. Kennedy was killed, his children were young. People worried about them. Congress said the Secret Service should protect Kennedy's family for two more years. In 1965, they made it four years. Later that same year, they made another change. A president and his or her spouse would be protected for the rest of their lives.

**DID YOU KNOW?**

In 2003, in a decision prompted by the 2001 attacks on the World Trade Center and the Pentagon, the Secret Service was moved from the Department of the Treasury to the Department of Homeland Security.

Agents and the people they protect often become close. President George W. Bush called one of his agents, Nick Trotta, by the nickname "Nicky." Bush's adviser Karl Rove always made sure the agents got something to eat while on duty. Unfortunately, Secret Service mistakes can **strain** that relationship. In 2009, two party crashers got into the White House. In 2014, a man got over the White House fence. He had a knife. He got into the White House by the north doors and ran to the East Room. Finally, he was stopped. In 2011, a bullet hit the White House. President Barack Obama's daughter Sasha was inside. The *Washington Post* wrote about First Lady Michelle Obama's response to the bullet. She was very angry. She criticized Secret Service director Mark Sullivan.

**strain:** to make tense or unfriendly

At speeches, debates, and other events, Secret Service agents survey the crowd for weapons and suspicious behavior.

FEDERAL MARSHALS

Deputy US Marshal Wyatt Earp became famous for an 1881 gunfight at the O.K. Corral in Tombstone, Arizona. He is pictured here in the middle of the front row.

# Introduction

A **federal** courtroom can be an unsafe place. People don't love being sent to jail. Sometimes, they attack judges. At other times, thieves turn on one another. In 1789, the US Marshals Service was created to protect the federal courts. US marshals, also called federal marshals, watch over court proceedings. They also take prisoners from one place to another. In 1971, the US Marshals Service began running the Witness Security Program. This program hides people who help catch criminals. These people might be in danger. They are given new identities and places to live. The program has kept more than 18,000 people safe. Marshals also hunt down people who commit federal crimes. They run the "Most Wanted" program. Sometimes, they bust a big criminal ring. The ring might have many valuable items. The marshals sell the art, jewelry, and cars. The money is given to victims. It also helps fund the work of the US Marshals Service.

In 1954, the Supreme Court ruled that separating schools by race was against the law. Federal marshals made sure schools followed the ruling.

## DID YOU KNOW?

In the United States, a federal crime is one that violates a law passed by the US Congress.

**federal:** relating to a national or central government

US officials say the Hells Angels are an organized crime gang involved in motorcycle theft and the drug trade.

# The Moment

In 1996, Carsten Stroud published a book called *Deadly Force: In the Streets with the US Marshals*. He describes how he followed the US Marshals Service's fugitive **apprehension** unit. Stroud says that in the 1990s, the marshals wanted to take down some violent bikers. The men were wanted on charges of murder, weapons smuggling, and **extortion**. They hung out at a bar in rural New York. The doors of the bar were locked. They were also made of steel. But a marshal named Grizzly Dalton had a plan.

**apprehension:** the capture and arrest of someone

**extortion:** to obtain something by using force or intimidation

The bikers were all in a motorcycle club called the Hells Angels. First, Grizzly tracked down a Hells Angel. This man was wanted for fleeing **felony** charges. Grizzly caught the man. Then he took the man's bike. He also took his clothes. Now, Grizzly could look like a Hells Angel. The clothes would be his ticket into the bar. When he got to the bar, he parked the man's bike. He banged on the door. Finally, he was let in. Grizzly lured the bikers into the parking lot, one by one. He told them he was having trouble with his bike. He asked if they would take a look. Once they were outside, Grizzly gave a signal. Other marshals jumped out from where they were hiding. They dragged each biker into the bushes. In the end, they cleared the entire bar.

**felony:** a serious crime that is punished by imprisonment for more than a year or by death

The Hells Angels bar that Grizzly Dalton raided was reinforced with concrete. There were also cameras and a motion detector to let them know when cops arrived.

# History of Order

The US Marshals Service is almost as old as the United States, and is still important today.

**1789**

George Washington appoints the first 13 federal marshals.

**1794**

Robert Forsyth is shot while delivering court papers in Augusta, Georgia. He is the first US marshal to be killed in the line of duty.

**1850–1861**

Federal marshals enforce the Fugitive Slave Law of 1850. They arrest runaway slaves and return them to plantations in the South.

**1877**

Frederick Douglass becomes the first African American US marshal.

**1960**

US marshals enforce the desegregation of an all-white school in Louisiana by escorting six-year-old African American student Ruby Bridges into the building.

**1970**

The Federal Air Marshal Service is created to combat the hijacking of planes.

**1973**

In Wounded Knee, South Dakota, federal marshals trade fire with members of the American Indian Movement (AIM). AIM demands the US government make good on treaties from the nineteenth and early twentieth centuries.

**1981**

The US Marshals Service creates Fugitive Investigative Strike Teams, or FIST. These teams look for violent fugitives. The first FIST team begins hunting down drug dealers in Miami, Florida.

**2001**

Federal marshals are first responders at the attacks on the World Trade Center in New York City and on the Pentagon in Washington, D.C.

**2016**

Nationwide, federal marshals average 273 arrests of fugitives a day.

With the help of other agencies, federal marshals tracked down 1,720 foreign fugitives in 2016.

# The Spread of Justice

A man in Paris robs a bank. A woman in Utah kidnaps a child. The bank robber flees to Salt Lake City. The woman takes the baby to France. US marshals track down both of them. US marshals do not have **jurisdiction** in other nations. They must work with foreign police to bring these criminals to justice. US marshals have offices in Mexico, Jamaica, and the Dominican Republic. They work with the border patrols of Canada and Mexico. They try to stop criminals from coming into or leaving the US. Some marshals work at Interpol. This is the International Criminal Police Organization. It connects forces from 190 countries.

**jurisdiction:** the legal authority to administer justice

US marshals try to get along well with foreign officials. They learn new languages and study other countries' customs. They must be sensitive to other cultures. Foreign officers come to the United States as well. They look for their own crooks. Marshals in the United States might help these officers get around. They might give them information or find them a place to stay. They might even suggest a good place to eat. This way, marshals can get help when they need it, too. Also, they know that foreign crooks might break the law in the United States. Victims of crime in all places need justice.

Federal marshals are on high alert when they patrol courts during high-profile trials.

## INTERNATIONAL CRIMINAL POLICE ORGANIZATION

In 1914, police officers and lawyers from 24 countries met in Monaco. This was the first International Criminal Police Congress. They talked about the methods police should use when arresting someone. They went over crime records. This was the beginning of Interpol. Today, Interpol helps police forces all over the world work together. Interpol honors the laws of each country. Each member country donates money to help fund the project. Interpol tracks international crime rings. Another priority is fighting acts of terrorism.

# Living Within the Law

The job of a US marshal is physically demanding. In a courtroom, it does not hurt to have muscles. A tough-looking marshal will make a prisoner think twice about attacking a judge. Most fugitives do not want to be caught. A marshal might have to wrestle a person to the ground. They might have to chase someone. A marshal also handles heavy equipment. They might carry an assault rifle. They might wield a battering ram. This is a tool used to bust down a door. Even a "mini" ram weighs 20 to 30 pounds (9 to 14 kilograms). For this reason, there are not many elderly marshals.

Applicants must be between 21 and 36 years old. They must pass a fitness test. Once they are marshals, they must pass this test each year. They cannot have serious health problems such as high blood pressure. In order to stay in shape, marshals get a lot of exercise. Many lift weights and run every day. They might do all this before they start work at 8:00 a.m. They do not want to lose any strength. They must keep up their **stamina**. A life might depend on it.

> **DID YOU KNOW?**
>
> One US marshal with great stamina was Chief Deputy Helen Crawford, who served on the force for 36 years.

**stamina:** the ability to exert physical or mental effort for a long period of time

Federal marshals must not have any health conditions that would prevent them from being able to run, fight, or stand for long periods of time.

# Conclusion

A law is only as strong as our ability to enforce it. Officers are the face of the law. They take it to the streets. There, they face danger. They also make tough moral choices. No one agrees with every law. At times, officers are asked to uphold laws they do not think are right or fair. Some US marshals did not want to hunt down slaves in the 1850s. Today, some members of law enforcement do not like new drug or civil rights laws. So each officer must decide what to do. If they choose to not uphold a law, the public might talk about it. This might bring about a change in the law. But these officers know they will also have to face penalties. The law can bind us all together only if no one is above it.

# Glossary

**apprehension:** the capture and arrest of someone

**assassination:** the murder of a person in a planned, secret attack, often for political reasons

**bandit:** an outlaw who lives by stealing from other people

**beat:** police terminology that means a territory and time that a police officer patrols

**bigotry:** hatred or intolerance toward the members of a particular group

**brutal:** extremely harsh or violent

**cavalry:** the division of an army that rides horses

**civil war:** a war between groups of people in the same country

**corruption:** dishonest behavior, especially of people in power

**counterfeiting:** the process of making a fake copy of something of value

**crook:** a person who gets what he or she wants in dishonest ways

**customs:** practices or acts common to a particular group of people

**extortion:** to obtain something by using force or intimidation

**fanfare:** a short and lively burst of music

**federal:** relating to a national or central government

**felony:** a serious crime that is punished by imprisonment for more than a year or by death

**fife:** a small flute often used in battle to give signals and orders to the troops

**identity fraud:** using someone else's personal information illegally, usually in order to get money

**immigrants:** people who come to a country to live there

**jurisdiction:** the legal authority to administer justice

**legacy:** a quality or tradition passed on from one generation to the next

**negotiate:** to try to solve an issue in a way that is acceptable to everyone

**peer pressure:** influence from other people in a group or community

**prestigious:** honored or having a high status

**recruit:** to encourage someone to apply for or to fill a position

**stamina:** the ability to exert physical or mental effort for a long period of time

**strain:** to make tense or unfriendly

**strike:** a protest in which a group of workers stop working in order to get their employer to agree to their demands

# Quiz

**1** In what year were the first watchmen established in Boston?

**2** Who ordered the creation of the first police force in New York City?

**3** Who is the founder of the Texas Rangers?

**4** Why did Mexican soldiers call the Texas Rangers *Los Diablos Tejanos* during the Mexican American War?

**5** Where are Secret Service members trained?

**6** In what year did the Secret Service begin protecting presidents from assassination?

**7** How many presidents had been killed before the Secret Service began protecting them?

**8** What were the US Marshals created to protect?

**8.** The federal courts

**7.** Three

**6.** 1901

**5.** The Federal Law Enforcement Training Center (FLETC) in Glynco, Georgia

**4.** They were known for being brutal and mean.

**3.** Stephen F. Austin

**2.** The governor of New York

**1.** 1631

# Index

# Selected Bibliography

Reppetto, Thomas A. *The Blue Parade*. New York: Free Press, 1978.

Spradlin, Michael P. *Texas Rangers: Legendary Lawmen*. New York: Walker & Company, 2008.

Stroud, Carsten. *Deadly Force: In the Streets with the U.S. Marshals*. New York: Bantam Books, 1996.

"Early police in the United States." *Encyclopædia Britannica Online*. Encyclopædia Britannica, n.d. Web. Accessed February 6, 2017. https://www.britannica.com/topic/police/Early-police-in-the-United-States/.

"Texas Rangers." Austin, TX: Texas Department of Public Safety, n.d. Web. Accessed February 6, 2017. https://www.dps.texas.gov/TexasRangers/.

U.S. Department of Homeland Security. Official Secret Service website. Washington, D.C.: United States Secret Service, n.d. Web. Accessed February 6, 2017. https://www.secretservice.gov/.

U.S. Department of Justice. Official U.S. Marshals website. Washington, D.C.: U.S. Marshals Service, n.d. Web. Accessed February 6, 2017. https://www.usmarshals.gov/.